Without Title

Without Title

GEOFFREY HILL

YALE UNIVERSITY PRESS   NEW HAVEN & LONDON

First published in the United States in 2007 by Yale University Press.
First published in the United Kingdom in 2006 by the Penguin Group.
Copyright © 2006 by Geoffrey Hill.
All rights reserved.
This book may not be reproduced, in whole or in part, including illustrations, in any form (beyond that copying permitted by Sections 107 and 108 of the U.S. Copyright Law and except by reviewers for the public press), without written permission from the publishers.

'La Bufera' by Eugenio Montale © Arnoldo Mondadori Editore, Milano

Set in 11/14.25 pt. Aldus by Rowland Phototypesetting Ltd., Bury St. Edmunds, Suffolk

Printed in the United States of America.

Library of Congress Control Number: 2006926124

A catalogue record for this book is available from the British Library.

The paper in this book meets the guidelines for permanence and durability of the Committee on Production Guidelines for Book Longevity of the Council on Library Resources.

ISBN 978-0-300-12176-6 (hardcover : alk. paper)
ISBN 978-0-300-12157-5 (pbk. : alk. paper)

10 9 8 7 6 5 4 3 2 1

in omaggio a
Eugenio Montale

Here to my mind is the objection to taking love as ultimate. There is no higher form of unity, I can agree. But we do not know love as the complete union of individuals, such that we can predicate of it the entirety of what belongs to them. And if we extend the sense of love and make it higher than what we experience, I do not see myself that we are sure of preserving that amount of self-existence in the individuals which seems necessary for love. F. H. BRADLEY

The profound nature will have a savage rudeness; the delicate one will be shallow, or the victim of sensibility; the richly accomplished will have some capital absurdity; and so every piece has a crack. 'Tis strange, but this masterpiece is a result of such an extreme delicacy, that the most unobserved flaw in the boy will neutralize the most aspiring genius, and spoil the work. R. W. EMERSON

Acknowledgements

The epigraphs for Section 2 ('Pindarics') are taken from Cesare Pavese, *This Business of Living: Diaries 1935–1950*, translated by A. E. Murch with Jeanne Molli, published by Quartet Books, London, 1980.

The epigraph on page 29 is from a song by Jimi Hendrix.

The epigraph on page 70 is the first line of Hart Crane's 'Reply'.

The epigraph on page 75 is from the film *The Spy in Black*, 1939, directed by Michael Powell, starring Conrad Veidt and Valerie Hobson.

Contents

1

Improvisation on 'O Welt ich muss dich lassen'

Traurig as one is between bearers, dancers,
old comrades from the Crem or at the Palais,
that's not the issue. Can't decide among
the cheap comedians. I do panic.
Queer noise going ón there like a gander
rehearsing its angry call. I long to stay
immortal and ageless, to stick around
for the Bacchantes' orgy, folk throwing up.
I had a dream in which this is all real,
where we rip off our masks and sing
'O Welt ich muss dich lassen'; medics on cue
for the recite-a-thon. Forget your science.
Dead friends are no remoter than in life.
It's curtains, though, protesting I can tell
limbo-dancers from wizards, chaps who tear
papers to shreds then flap them as by magic
back in one piece, *You're fired* still crisp, pristine.

Without Title
to PMH

Pheromones moribund, but something other
bemuses mourning, more than vows unmade,
shared life aborted. I could write at length
an entailed history, the character
of unfruition, match my fellow townsman,
his grief's pastmaster though long-since cold,
culling the bay bowers to which he
cannot return. His gall his gift,
his sign a bloom-struck cherry bough; ours
flowering currant that close-to stinks of cat.
Ingenuous I recall us, a genius
for misconception making our divorced
selves of love still agelessly at one:
no restitution but with wired laurels.

Chromatic Tunes

Each waking I conclude erotic dreams
private mass entertainment. There's
no joy in this, nor do I spend desire
that things should be so. Otherwise I read
of matrimony on your foreign planet
but cannot find the language. Otherwise
featureless idling strews the wintry strands;
woods bare their clutter; sea birds appear
to boister with the waves, to wrench themselves
windborne. The soughing moon-tide's hulkingness,
massive passivity, works its gnarls of light.
Further I cannot judge
whether to go, or stay; or tell how one
might stay, another go, far flung, bereft.

In Ipsley Church Lane 1

More than ever I see through painters' eyes.
The white hedge-parsleys pall, the soot is on them.
Clogged thorn-blossom sticks, like burnt cauliflower,
to the festered hedge-rim. More than I care to think
I am *as one* coarsened by feckless grief.
Storm cloud and sun together bring out the yellow of stone.

But that's lyricism, as Father Guardini
equably names it: autosuggestion, mania,
working off a chagrin close to despair,
ridden by jealousy of all self-healed
in sexual love, each selving each, the gift
of that necessity their elect choice.

Later, as in late autumn, there will be
the mass-produced wax berries, and perhaps
an unearthed wasps' nest like a paper skull,
where fragile cauls of cobweb start to shine.
Where the quick spider mummifies its dead
rage shall move somnolent yet unappeased.

The Jumping Boy

1

Here is the jumping boy, the boy
who jumps as I speak.

He is at home on the king's highway,
in call of the tall house, its blind
gable end, the trees – I know this place.

The road, on broad contourings drawn out of sight,
stops – wherever – but not at Lyonnesse,
though from Lyonnesse I shall bring you,

through grimed orchards, across gorse-hummocked
old common land everywhere given back
to the future of memory.

2

He leaps because he has serious
joy in leaping. The girl's

eyes no way allowed for, or else
she is close in covert and we
are to know that, not knowing how.

I'll bet she worships his plebeian
bullet head, Hermes' winged
plimsolls, the crinkled toy tin hat

held on by elastic. He is winning
a momentous and just war
with gravity.

3

This may be levitation. I
could do that. Give my remembrance
to his new body. These episodes occur.

4

Jump away, jumping boy; the boy I was
shouts go.

On the Reality of the Symbol

1

That he feared death – Karl Rahner – unrevealing.
Fine theologian with or against
the world, in senses that are not the world's,
his symbolism, both
a throwback and way forward, claims its own
cussedness, yet goes with the mystery.
Parturition of psalm like pissing blood
I múst say, the formal evidence
so much an issue. Though not painful
pain's in the offing, somewhere signifies
its needled presence. Plus, the prostate's
a nasty beast even at the best of times.
But for translation the old linguaduct
works not too badly. This is a translation.

2

So? Say it again: ephemeralities
ever recurring. There are numerous
things you can't speak or think. Must confess I
sometimes raped her ghost? The olive trees
oblige with well-reft branches. Scapegoats are not
hunted but driven out. There yet remain
impassioned and strange readings: a remote
cry of the blood sugars.
Try *melos* for desired numbness of breath.
And you a poet in all justice. Too
many signs: call scourings from fouled pipes
purification. There! the white dove plumps
her spectral finery. Building my ark begins
late in the terminal welter of the flood.

3

Pity love could not act us. No scarcity
of drama schools where Í live. In some of them
refusal's not much worse than other failings
I won't elaborate. We refused each other:
loss is what we are left with. Re-audition.
They'd take us back, instruct us to be old.
Here's bargain-gelt to move things on a stage.
More than a sexy trial a *Trauerspiel*
needs make-believe to launch the sordid fact.
Does this miscast us as a tragic chorus?
Can't answer that, I'm working on my role.
Shyster's from a Yiddish word for shit.
It's not, you know.
This is late scaffold-humour, turn me off.

4

On vision as a mode of neural tort:
and I could find myself becoming
overseer for rehabilitation,
imprinting with due licence the late-cancelled
stanzas that hymn roulette. Everything mortal
has to give from life. When we're exhausted
by ill-willing, the fictions of our joys,
violin, pleach-toned harp, and grand piano
melodize; the contessa's niece
glitters her gift three lengths of the salon.
Symbol burns off reality: take *The Red Shoes* –
since I'm to show beholden – how for instance
those awkward, svelte, death-struck life enhancers
labour their immortality proclaimed.

5

Gold, silver, to gel-blaze the dark places.
Black has its own gleam. Pascal's
name is a blank to many people; so
also are yours and mine.
There must be unnamed stars but all are numbered
de profundis. Check these on the web
spun by their own light. And does such knowledge
firm up allegiance to the stoic heavens?
And is the question real or rhetorical
when finally the all-or-nothing man
presses his wager? Such extravagance
here to expand on, to elect chaos
where there's a vacancy and peradventure
if chaos is the word.

6

The work of mourning – the *Trauerarbeit* –
bugles dead achievements. Regardless
and in spite of, what a memory
fenced by glittering breakage. Stabs
at the long jump (juniors) from a mired run up,
off a fractured board. Five seconds' freedom
I nominate to be the normal freedom
of the mob-ruled. Subsequent fables,
men of stale will nursing their secret wounds,
the token of the scarecrow as sufferer,
seem done for. Death fancies us but finally
leaves us alone. Metaphysics remain
in common language something of a joke.
Mourning my meaning is what I meant to say.

Insert Here

Fuit d'une fuite éternelle – no, founded
in eternal light. And then what?

. . .

A clash of trodden ashes, if clinker
can be called ashes.

. . .

                    The angular
sun on windows or windshields like swans
taking off and alighting.

. . .

Let me be, says the dying man, let me fall
upwards toward my roots.

Tu B'Shevat

Returning to my own green winter, dense
invocation and slow-growing charge
unlike anywhere: Hebrew alone will serve

this narrative which is a broken thing –
because I cannot well pronounce it
interpreter, mage, teller of righteousness.

Word for the sun found here six-pronged and noble.

The real tree being the almond, the land
Israel, the voice prophetically enlarged,
the end, so far conceived and unprepared for,

absolves witness.

2

Not much to go for there. I can remit you
endurances at worst or transfer funds
on estimates of cost. Subsistence-wrung

and royal Hebrew – *to the chief musician* –
suffering servant, plenitude that mourns,
singer of griefs unsung, the aleph-tav

of others' fruits and vines. Moshe Dayan,
en route to Suez, praised the flourishing
Palestinian date-harvest –

which was not to the purpose. I salute purpose:
festivals where they strip the vital groves,
attune their joy and wish nobody harm.

Children's Games

From laughter to slaughter,
from shul to Sheol,
from Torah to Ahor.
Say Noah-Shoah.
Noah-Shoah! Noah-Shoah!
Tell Bialik.

. . .

The air foil-fêted
and with zinc clatterings,
each new gust slaps
the wire-strung small
neighbourhood flags into wind-
milling windmills.

. . .

For this day and for dread
of Sheol, let the dead remain
under sedation.
These are memory games.
Find Bialik,
he should know.

To Lucien Richard: On Suffering

The undulant road makes the way-out tide
rise and fall. After the merchants' houses
the tarred fishing shacks and places that sell bait;
after the shade trees the gleaned reaches of sand.
Sea-bass are plentiful. Although the smallest
get thrown back – legal – they mostly die,
float for a short while, scales catching the sun.

———

Granite plugs through sand bluffs. The stub
lighthouses resemble follies or summer homes
for checkerboard painters. Gulls appear
laggard and yet they are sleekly primed.
The fine machinery of instinctual natures
is well adjusted to the environment,
hooks up arrivals to the thermal tower.

———

I take on Seneca, could have sung like Jonah
at your discretion. So enjoyed it when
the weighted line you cast tore from its rod,
bait and all, and flippered and was gone,
the timing perfect, perfect your chagrin-
charged resignation, mute expressive glare:
no chance to practise custody of the eyes.

———

So I said to them half-blinded which
of you is the angel? And which angel?
I did not think there were angels. The sea
light was visionary, as it sometimes is
to susceptible people. Dead or alive
we sojourn in the world's refuge and abattoir.
Pity about the tackle. I could have wept.

Wild Clematis in Winter
i.m. William Cookson

Old traveller's joy appears like naked thorn blossom
as we speed citywards through blurry detail –
wild clematis' springing false bloom of seed pods,
the earth lying shotten, the sun shrouded off-white,
wet ferns ripped bare, flat as fishes' backbones,
with the embankment grass frost-hacked and hackled,
wastage, seepage, showing up everywhere,
in this blanched apparition.

Offertorium: December 2002

For rain-sprigged yew trees, blockish as they guard
admonitory sparse berries, atrorubent
stone holt of darkness, no, of claustral light:

for late distortions lodged by first mistakes;
for all departing, as our selves, from time;
for random justice held with things half-known,

with restitution if things come to that.

Epiphany at Hurcott

Profoundly silent January shows up
clamant with colour, greening in fine rain,
luminous malachite of twig-thicket and bole
brightest at sundown.

On hedge-banks and small rubbed bluffs the red earth,
dampened to umber, tints the valley sides.
Holly cliffs glitter like cut anthracite.
The lake, reflective, floats, brimfull, its tawny sky.

Epiphany at Saint Mary and All Saints

The wise men, vulnerable in ageing plaster,
are borne as gifts
to be set down among the other treasures
in their familial strangeness, mystery's toys.

Below the church the Stour slovens
through its narrow cut.
On service roads the lights cast amber salt
slatted with a thin rain doubling as snow.

Showings are not unknown: a six-winged seraph
somewhere impends – it is the geste of invention,
not the creative but the creator spirit.
The night air sings a colder spell to come.

Discourse: For Stanley Rosen

1

As to whether there persists – enlighten me –
a dialectic: labour into desire.
Forgive my small vocabulary that tries
and abides your patience. What a wonder's
man the philosopher set on his throne.
What a wonder he is, and how
abysmal. I would not have you say
I speak ungratefully; or that there's self
going spare in our unsparing tribute.
Arbeitsknecht by adoption, I never
hurl down advice, even to shake the building.
Perhaps (but not likely) I may be still
a whizz at ordinary language and you
mishear things.

2

No, put it this way: cancel, expunge, annul,
self-reference. Philosophy keeps up
embarrassment and expense. I'd quit us
of further scars had these now been incurred.
You're magisterial in judgement's gorge
where the rocks are at all angles and the stream
huggers its way through:
let's flip with self-projection's paper boat.
Language not revealing to the elect
only; and wild descenders pierced by good.
So few of us absolved when what we write
sets us to rights on some scale of justice.
You're magisterial in your own conviction.
And a clown with it, and a judge of clowns.

3

Susurrations of winter: voicing stems mistune
a glass harmonica at my good ear.
The alien's close to home, the changeling's not
too much a prodigy or wastrel; lovers
and children not inimical by rote.
Something here even so. Our well dug-in
language pitches us as it finds –
I tell myself
don't wreck a good phrase simply to boost sense –
granted its dark places, the fabled burden;
its loops and extraordinary progressions;
its mere conundrums forms and rites of discourse;
its bleak littoral swept by bursts of sunlight;
its earthen genius auditing the spheres.

In Ipsley Church Lane 2

Sage-green through olive to oxidized copper,
the rainward stone tower-face. Graveyard
blossom comes off in handfuls – the lilac
turned overnight a rough tobacco brown.
Every few minutes the drizzle shakes
itself like a dog:

substantially the world as is, its heavy body
and its lightnesses emblems, a glitter
held in keel-shaped dock leaves, varieties
of sameness, the pebbles I see sing
polychrome under rainwash,
arrayed in disarray, immortal raiment:

my question, since I am paid a retainer,
is whether the appearances, the astonishments,
stand in their own keepings finally
or are annulled through the changed measures of light.
Imagination, freakish, dashing every way,
defers annulment.

Improvisations for Jimi Hendrix

Somewhere a Queen is weeping
Somewhere a King has no wife

1

I am the chorus and I urge you
act messenger's idiom from Greek tragedy.
Get to know words like the gods'
inconstant anger.

Stand in for Pasiphaean bull,
exquisite player of neumes!
Enlarge the lionized
apparatus of fucking,
Wacko falsetto of stuck pig.

You can vibe self-defector and know
how to project
Olympian light waves.

The show guitar melts like sealing wax.
It mutes and scalds. Your fingers
burning secrets.

Your legerdemain.

Extraordinary progressions chart
no standard progress.

Call guru noises inc gk.
There is no good ending admits fade-out.

By rights you shall have
top prize longevity
wiped as a gift.

2

Prime time, whole time, the planet's
run by toupée'd pinkoes: but not ruled.
Not even music rules.

What kind contortions fix hex-mind pyrewise?

Something unexplained – I exempt his music.

No huckster, then, dazed gambler with real grace,
saved possibly; and the hotel rooms
destroyed themselves.

3

Short-changed and on short time let us
walk óh-so óh-so with all new gods.
Showmen kill shaman, dunk parts in late

wag-chat's petty shrine. I had a line all
set to go; a lien now. Even the shadow-
death cues further shadows. Take his hand,
Medea, if he can find it. *Lysergic*

also is made up Greek.

4

Sometimes the king of a forbidden country
has his entitlement, his lineage,
adorned by error.

Somehow a king delivers his true bride
in the perilous
marsh of childbirth and all three go safe.

Yes there is weeping and yes some find
the lost miracle and do not know it;

swagger royally, play the pretender
to sinking Atlantis,
drown in their star-dust. Some are reborn.

. . .

Somewhere the slave is master of his desires
and lords it in great music
and the children dance.

2 Pindarics
after Cesare Pavese

1

What, then, can you deny this most hateful of men? You can deny him nothing whatsoever.

Convenes and prospers, being espoused
neither to bag-lady, nor yet to enraged
flamenco-dancer; untargeted by fishwife;
no crosslegged succubus, no unfitted
scrapping-bitch his barren mate.
Yet lust's the ground of wedlock, even sublimed
like alcohol in a stew. And mutual comfort
rides on the pelvic bone. As Ces says,
you can deny him nothing. Nothing,

when in the counterturn all is absurd:
as postures to be held, to be beheld –
I'm running a slight fever: anniversaries
unman me – meeting only substance,
finishing against the clock, in swive
and swive about, begetter of sexed skin.
Plea-bargainer for annulment by return.
I, the lost soul of taste; he a provider
of differentials, calculated stress.

Stand here: the passing wonder's not to age.
Bristol-bound diesel, under Brunel's roof
burring the air violet with its exhaust.
Best to ignore his eye – he's marked us though –
and well-hung barathea, period flares.

The political body does not die and so does not have to
answer for itself before any God.

Nomen or *numen* when you meant *nomos*.
But at this juncture the strophe stands
incontrovertibly revealed, exact,
with *bonum simplex* and like *civitas*,
talismanic in the microchip,
power not to descend to the thing done,
the garbling utile. Chronically discharged
that stream slurs among spoil-heaps, low and thick
and all-tenacious. Cranking forgotten skills

there must be – somewhere – choices that succeed,
all elements unarguably of that phase.
People go shuttery like on a sub
splayed in a crash-dive –
so keep in trim, you and your cheated oppo,
is my advice before I take this hand.
Though refutation's a lost cause at best,
the body politic that does not die
and is not answerable to any God,

returns a kind of grandeur on the shame.
Power's not everyplace that mood is,
and anarchy by files deploys to order
as if through modes of conduct or of weight,
dactyls advancing against a contrived rest.

3

Pf!!!!

Weddings break mirrors, make stale blossoms,
vex feats of memory and feast vexation.
The house of appearances is briefly possessed.
I do not asset such debts however.
Narrowly, luck and mischance, I owe you my life
of imagination and have sod-all
to show for it but egregious powers,
remote animation, noiseless bolt-lightning,
zagging Twenties-style film chalk-labelled *Thinks*;

or, *Again you are ours, lost beauty of the world*;
or, *The mystery inheres and is not nothing*;
or, *Untie the rope – quick, now scarper, sauve
qui peut*, which is a bad wish but a good
omen from a malign siesta. Rapid
eye movements, touch of paralysis, sign
everybody asleep. There is too great
eagerness for sleep unites the undisposed.
How different from robust motel films. I

could not have imagined this achievement
except by repossessing fifty years.
Such were your lineaments and I missed you,
dare I say, *lord of life*. Dissertations
will stand famous in which we go unnamed.

4

The secret of an artistic creation eludes its creator until the
very moment when the solution strikes him.

This could be you or me, Cesare; you're
the second most self-centred man I know,
though at the far edge nothing if not staunch.
Women also are lords of life. With some
I act Pluto to Ceres, take protégés
of light and shadow. With some I beget
inestimable children of the mind,
a wag, a karaoke on the house.
Erotic reality, Tasso's chariot,

engages the new strophe. Time is something
because of what's tossed out by paradox.
Nothing is timeless, let be satisfied
with baffled wordplay crowding to the life,
align catastrophe by chance pursued.
Limelight excites the rabble, shows them tricks,
the prancing orchestra of self-disgust.
Too much is theatre by all accounts,
the scrim, and curtain, and proscenium arch.

Retail the coda well before due date
had better be the motto of my choice.
Hand me the doubtful laurel and we'll find
how well its legend caters to the dead;
taking our bow, confuse ourselves with fame.

5

But of course 'to go toward the people' was part of the
catastrophe. And then weren't we too the people?

Not to fiddle overmuch with words,
if there is wit enough pindarics turn
right from the start; the counterturn shall set
us straight, justly, in the path of power:
with ramps for breakout, impotence, dismay,
our strength our weakness our recrimination.
The packs are gathering chattered in fierce code,
I'd happily trade 'Enigma' for the crib
of a sealed vow declared opened by love.

So much I've read you in the new language
we could do it together. Turning towards
the people is no worse, no better, say,
than chancre of exile. Let us have
the roving taste that lingers among spice
whether of women or the laureate's rack,
élite conjunction with the mob's own lords,
the push-and-pull of predicate acclaim;
compassion sold, mislaid, become an art.

This said for origins; résumés are not
on charge lightly to resume things. Still,
I backed a terse epode to clue us in:
some rig of question that is just as much
an affirmation – weren't we too the people?

6

I now understand the writers of the Augustan age much
better, and no longer impulsively call Ovid a clown.

A strigil for my eczema (pleurolepidid
of pool-chlorine). Stark as I am, the rubs
of nerve stay more or less as I swam her.
Swimming's good for the heart, the heart is good
for perhaps next session. There are questions
made not to be answered. I can't ask them,
not only of myself. What is psoriasis
in the eternal economy? I have a rapt
ambition towards which I fetch my strength.

You were a swimmer, Ces, and with a style,
or so I trim your wake who never saw you.
Well-kept release of life, the body-lagged
spirit, was that element's figuration.
Women are a contagious abstinence.
What's this strophe against? It must have heard
something beyond talk of byronic charm.
Abstinence isn't the right word; nor is
contagious. Meanwhile my writing fingers weep.

Ovid would have our number, definitely.
Look at yourself, it makes no difference
that the mirror is upside down. Judicial
stay on writ won at eleventh hour
changes nothing. Small hotels are to die in.

We discovered Italy – this is the point – seeking the men
and the words in America, Russia, France and Spain.

Moves to embarrass you with waning stock –
but I prevaricate. Applied eugenics
essentially: a language won and wrought
for the conglomerate that is called a nation.
Disputed beyond tolerance of affront
in migrants' habitations; hunkered down
next to the speechless word, the unworded seer.
Transported with mishandling; yet the rest
sad entertainers lined up for the cull.

Poetry's a public act by long engagement.
I've run myself against it; if inured
the spikier the better, my old blood!
Begloried, sheer of state, armed by the sea.
All-funding eloquence the shallow leach,
the curiosities – bones from Leviathan
with a wrenched hook or two, and jewelled eyes.
Bravo, our constitution of report,
and barren empire basking on its tides.

Rejection turns an option for the will,
affective or elective as it comes;
and affirmation stands denial's twin.
I found myself
other than finding her ǀ my other voice.

8

When a woman smells of sperm and it is not mine,
I don't like it.

Typical as comedians – something lewd
slips from your homework-journal to my hand,
sticks like a noxious treat in silver paper.
Disasters have their triumphs: redeemed swots,
you with your Whitman, while I cribbed from much
maligned beau Allen Tate pindaric odes.
Narrative's easy – up we go and down –
except I feel a bounder to myself.
Now, thát ís yóu, Ces, sullen and alert.

Observe those sprung stresses, five in a row:
here's English fór you, Hopkins' bastard classic.
Nasty, I fell for love it stands to say.
She kept me on the spot like nothing else
given our schooling. Centre of the World
(film of that title; credits rolling up).
I can't do better now than hunt a phrase,
old mystic howler clutching at the note.
You too a truth-freak in your famous lair

know as you must a burden in the main
unbearable. Quires of bad music left
after the band's barged past for the last time;
the band-room sweat, the marches stacked askew,
the clarion yard at gaze, the crowd dispersed.

Poetry is repetition. Calvino has cheerfully arrived to tell
me this.

Not to unthink the work done – but a dervish
whirlstorm of sepia and sand
occludes us, like a twister on the bed
of a shallow sea. Cuttlefish bones are found
incongruously – not here their own sea-grottoes –
in parrots' cages or in books of verse.
Seashells are more elaborate and hiss,
tell childhood fortunes, voyage from Madagascar.
Nothing outsmarts or dulls the unsleeping self

pity that's pitiless even to itself.
A shadow heaps more umbrage than these words
an old soubrette drinks to deaf memory,
roaming fancy's club. Others might brag
admission charge is the true price of fame;
all else subvention, bonuses, blithe fraud.
What did the Strega pull? It bought no women –
by which I judge these things – no life
out of harm's way. Nor did it crown a gift

timely, immortal, dummied-up like death.
As if who knew? The pacified distraught?
Repetition betrays us, our minds at odds
in lassitude, diremption, the absurd vice,
of contradictions and of dictions contra.

The eternal falsity of poetry is that its events occur in a
time that differs from reality.

La bufera – the storm – yes but in whose
memory am I to raise up this storm,
establish tides of scattery impaction,
e altro, and so on? They say the autumn comet
'presages disasters' as portents of our art
more than ever Montale's. If he requires
authorization I shall finger him
amid the sodden trajectories of blind sycamore.
Ces, and I have this also in good faith,

could read presages and lately grew uncanny
as a wild goat grows cunning on the cliffs.
There is a snag here that I still can't fathom.
Epigraphs too are elusive. From whose depth
shall I type-code this storm? It feels good
raising the question that can sound at once
heroic and perplexed. Gizmo remains
the heroic line, includes my dental plate,
spittle spunk-thick, gamy fermenting breath.

Storms at first light our drummers. You
shall outlive the next century,
fatalities allowed for. Can't go further
unless to claim I found such plenitude
one of the dark moon's non-existent seas.

You have had the fruitful idea that destiny is myth.

Thinking this through, there is the structure
of choric stance or stanza, the final stand.
Anyone can be chorus; it is not
a matter of possession but of station,
of good form even. Station is given
not only in this book: mailmen go choric
as much as ever; likewise the harmless crank,
the prescient doomed passenger. Macbeth
attacks front-stage his drubly visioning.

I think catastrophe; feel, touch, stasis
wholly without stillness. The pilot scans
into the nimbus of his utmost fix;
an ancient *anabasis*, lift of pride.
The 30s look I stiff for some cause; or else,
again, there's evidence not to be plumbed.
I can't say more as yet, the hurtling agent
fixed in mind's body, a last steadying beam:
'*I* is an other'. Grand tautologies

the symmetries of chaos. There's a form
of innocence with which we play the end,
that thrives by various names including guilt,
spitted on entertainment: outside film
the busiest stuntmen are the torturers.

The artist labours under restrictions that will be valueless in
the eyes of posterity.

Lateness is palpable and I no longer
read in the expectation of chance greatness
as formerly I hoped for blurred encounters
transforfeiting my life.
How strange you have to be to stay faithful.
I've little patience, sometimes a sign of cunning,
though more than you had. Let's trade names,
Mr Toad, Dante; stake the high deal its chance
as citizens of some neophyte republic.

Yet where I am in this I simply o-
mitted to discover. Walked past the check-in
where they give you the stamped cards. Politic power
was the good Tudor term and stood for something.
But this is Johnny English. Animated,
a late extra perks his unwanted bits,
fails to win through.
Trash that headline found on the pantechnicon
metro: *Undefeated. Throws in the towel.*

Finally I want out (of Amor, Roma),
my friends only the stolid Piedmontese
kind enough not to notice. Trick I've noticed:
a wind turning trees to different contours
yet the same way.

If there is any human figure in my poetry, it is that of a
truant running back, full of joy, to his own village.

You shall be that naïf, yr mistress-soul
each month a pregnant blank. You, carry on
sombre litigation with the body of language.
And we will bring a verdict against you both,
both in law and the common voice. Pronounce
nem. con. though claquing our vacant jury.
I take it my pitch catches the emphasis
more by breathing than by contagion. Such
Fury's best occulted, non è vero?

But for those fifty years there are bailed crimes
bearing my words to Eros and to Equity
without warning or favour. Nail them on the gate
of the Old Vicarage; everyone passes there –
Lord Austin, Bill Morris, Mr Wyndham Shire,
the county almoner; farmer Giles with his
dourly-watered milk, the rag-and-bottle,
Jonah and Job, a line of cretin children
who thus go down to history unreprieved.

Our explainings are slipshod, sliding in the blood
of mutual offences, ignorance
and self-ignorance. I mean hers and mine.
You other selves, go back to playing dumb,
dumb but not dead, not fair, not ever final.

The work we achieve is always something other than
we intended.

Labour is allowed beauty and enhanced
beauty is labour of a kind. Democracy
not a bad word though even so much disliked
by the old rhetors and keen men of state.
Wish I could get my Greek fixed. Some heroes
were self-neutered one way or another,
not reckoning the bourse nor held possessed
by plutophotonics. Agoraphobia trades
fear of the market. Cry for Goethe's light.

Spin this like a thimble on a needle's end,
waiting for work: I've entered self-discharged.
Lately Propertius understood the power
of sexual politics – as Ovid did not
save by experience or its equivalent.
Ventriloquy's in, an esteemed project:
the élite is a smaller crowd,
you must accept this as I must. The best
song studies the gyre and is steadied by it.

I'm spent, signori, think I would rather
crash out than glide on through. Pound glided
through his own idiocy; in old age
fell upon clarities of incoherence,
muteness's epigrams, things crying off.

All this is without a doubt sincere, and unfortunately
entangled with the need for expression which his poetic
nature demands.

It would be good to snarl their *passages*
of vision, just for rag-week. Dear female chum,
in the freeze-frame of your perpetually
falling débris, pray for me. Did I ever
take you without a dryness? It is hard,
now, to ask that. The ornatures
of salutation fade. Nevertheless
this is how work gets done. What to attempt
is a bastard art revived – like formal curses

sputtering off through laughter. You can read me
almost too well; the labour to explain
not taken for concession by demand
but even so demanded. Love being love
in its thwart ways, almost to be preferred
because the groan's familiar, I give you back
such solace, dint for dint and, so perplexed,
expression must suffice, sometimes high-pitched
beyond much bearing. Pause for collection

and for chorale-like music, words over,
that is, superimposed. The tokens of their gods
lie scattered as they spun, as self-survivors
left them with such a haul: Amor, Cupiditas,
pacing the final act, friends heaped in drag.

Shakespeare was conscious of a double or treble reality
fused together into one line or a single word.

Say, Coriolanus fought from dark to dark,
a thing of blood. Not what I had in mind.
He could turn cities ashen being devoured
by his brain-dragon-worm, scarred travesty,
bespoke himself a dragon in a fen,
a *lonely* dragon – and he wás alone.
But hitting that one word, that swipe of rage,
blood-tears by nature, indenturing power,
Shakespeare's, not his, P. spilled out sex and fame.

Add that: our man was exiled to twelve months
of dire self-catering at Brancaleone.
Musso's block-strutters pinned him in their charts,
marked for a leftie, as indeed he was,
war-wounded one might say, asthma and cockroaches,
the hard sea-bathing. Also, they tortured Ginzburg
and Ginzburg died. That was another time.
I have some feeling for his widow's brusqueness.
The moment and the year commend the fact.

P. was not of that kind and took quarter,
spoke under flags of truce with his despair.
He hectored boys to fight then swanned away
on a prolonged vacation. This I got
out of a cried-up book. It may be true.

Another of his memorable sayings is 'all or nothing' –
'Aut Caesar aut nihil' – P. never stops halfway.

Need to see proof that P. slid Coriolanus
through to Italia; whether he admired him.
If hated, for what reason or whatever
runs off the track of reason. He was a *Lear* man
(I do know that) possibly thanks to Melville.
Cocteau filmed *Coriolanus*: this I've not seen
but want P. to have seen it, early enough.
Some say he was a traitor to himself,
slinking out of the race, and other jimjams.

Treason against the self is something I
can go along with, in lame kinds of ways.
In P.'s own case this could have been the missed
rite de passage or, worse than missing, botched –
the civil war and him not riding on it.
That sissiness he has, close to the nub.
Lear is too easy, the puréed madness
a kind of parity with the mad crime,
the self-willed absence from his royal self.

For Coriolanus there is no escape
in the sublime, in God, or melancholy,
no music for his state, no martyrdom,
no reconciling with the truth of things;
but, crazy-passive, a last mêlée of spite.

Fundamentally the fine arts and letters did not suffer under
fascism; cynically accepting the game as it was.

The nature it seems of that intelligence
is to be compromised. But, then, nothing is pure.
P. (Ces) blamed Ruskin for the fascist state.
Intrinsic value's at the root of this,
it can branch either way. So take your hook
and prune among the vine-steads, clever man,
humanity your skill, such as we are.
Ulisse, Ulisse, son io. Pound
was a Ruskinian, so it works out, so it

fits and sits fair to being plausible;
which is our métier. Promenade the baroque
divas and the god-haunched castrati.
The presence of the intrinsic's not in doubt,
the modus is. Now cue for oxymoron
that sounds – rocks – as a Monteverdi choir
is expected to, in íts joyous lament.
Intrinsic virtue's weighted by the elect;
is, first-last, for the people. This I maintain

since proof stays out of court. I wish you joy
in your post-pill amazement, P. (or Ces),
such audience for forgiveness as attends.
Self-reconciling anyone's afterthought
to the prescription slapped against your name.

To create a work is therefore to make absolute one's own
time, one's own space.

How reconciled was Ovid by such time
as in Vorónezh he was no man's fool?
I'm speaking brutally; the answer holds
in the way that vines hold, or a sloth
holds to the branch if this has been provided,
or like the skein of talk of my invention
misfocused here. In the neighbour's yard
tyres creak, slurp, on gravel; the yard door splits
into two parts . . . the answer from the question.

The question's lost while answers are to hand.
What P. describes – *duration of real pain* –
spikes with its radicals the roots of thought.
In Hebrew word and thing, the acting word –
the basic punning language though not all
punsters are poets, nor could they wish to be.
The absolute's absolution is itself.
For us – the brickmakers – Pharaonian time,
the sphinx's part-decipherable face.

Vorónezh: Ovid thrusts abruptly wide
the ice-locked shutters, discommodes his lyre
to Caesar's harbingers. Interrogation,
whatever is most feared. Truth's fatal vogue,
sad carnifex, self-styled of blood and wax.

*But the real, tremendous truth is this: suffering serves no
purpose whatever.*

Someone there has made a chalk drawing
of the common man. In history-time
he came and went so patient he was blind,
blinded, even, a tommy on Somme duckboards;
and his patience was brought against him,
a servitude ór an indictment.
If what I grope for lies above the mud-lid
we shall at some point grasp his calvary.
Other than the story this tells nothing –

small improvement on a child's stick figure
but not of that genre. It is named being
up against it, granted a token life,
reason or conscience if not libido
and may retort, even, with maimed
truth-telling, obscene gibberish. Rouault
could do it justice in black and white
this side of Revelation; or just about.
Other than the story this tells, nothing.

No courage can do more. There is a gap:
let us pass through it; the many voices –
of peasants and soldiers – are reinstated,
the pageants move, stooping, to hallow them.
Nothing tells this story of thee or another.

All these lamentations are far from stoical. So what?

After the prize-giving the valedictions;
after the phone call a brief sense
of what happiness would be like; after
the forgiveness a struggle to forgive.
Some discourse is expansive, but some
composed of opposing blocks. Again
the award ceremony as paradigm
for the expected. She gives herself
to the right man. Their painless composure.

But, to my purpose, the other, the choice
that is arbitrary, of the free will,
moving the unkeyed sections until they lock.
Not to deflect the wildest things; acceptance
a distinct willing; a reach for truth
like sentences from Tacitus at worst.
Delirium of order. Nor is this easy,
but music seems an answer, undisturbed
by other than itself, the keyed answer.

Or crystallography which I
think I misunderstand; it's not Stendhal.
Patterns of lines, mostly, raw in appearance.
I see I've defined a poem. Something I'd say
held over, deep in reserve, so that it may strike.

3

To the Teller of Fortunes

I

Spread sand not straw. Salt useless here although
useful elsewhere. Stresses count in a line,
help weld and wield. Take me to task – or worse –
for misappropriation. Pontoon's not
bridge: I understand that by reproof.
Plain speaking still an order I believe.
To which now add: the omens
blood-fuddled and in other ways befouled.
Sounds good.

II

Pointedly they drew daggers in the air.
More to the point he had recast
their programme of intent.
                            More to the point
they stalled the racketing old flail-tank saved
for tyrannicide –
but point taken: to let the children cross.

III

Morbidity thrives. Tiberius' emerald
greening the ulcer-finger.
Observer at the feast of infamy, your
choice abstentions. Stiff place card at table,
carte de visite, the plain memorial card,
redeem a quality of need, the twelve
pearl-handled fruit knives, the figs' entrails,
writs of departure served from the epergne.

(59)

IV

Well-taught articulation
                    and the Fates
past all necessity frivolous;
each doll so I jointed it moves dis-
jointedly, mime-shocked, smiling.

V

And then they cart us off which is not good,
not good, mea Hostia; so that we lose
sight of our selves before Lethe annuls us.
No more of us without whom there is nothing.

VI

Hail Caesar and the rest. Reviewing language
I am wrought up by how patient it is.
Even in Thule the durability
of light over a century – you
can rely on it, it augurs well.

VII

Chancy but promising. Who's that poet
tarred his horsewhip on aesthetes?
                            If this is just
thirteen syllables I shall survive.

Ex Propertio

Encouraged by a glib-tongued haruspex
to practise divination – what's wrong here?
Soothsayers hold their skills inviolate.
Incited by a renegade conjurer
I bowelled my loyalties to law and love
rhetorical in parts. Love as a necromant
re-infiltrates the dead *whilst* law usurps
upon itself: two elder shades of weight,
authority mere power, power in authority.
The act of love surpassing eloquence –
a shadow there of Amor in his stride.
I shan't recover divination's charm
out of these studs and hooks or Hymen's ring
of decayed iron, or cauterizing brand.

Ars
i.m. Ken Smith

1

Hazardous but press on. Enjambment
drags: hinge of induration
not a patent success.
Comparisons build tautologies yet again.
What is incomparable and are we
making a list?

Don't lay destructive charge if you were booked
for exhibition.
To confess mayhem plead ornate regard.
Ciceronian conclusions, fixed resolve.

Style paradox inertia's mobile face
for the duration. It has been thought
expedient to have us curse and weep
with the same countenance as one inspired.

Delete *delenda est* – exemplary
Carthage her rubbed-in wounds.
Not everything's a joke but we've been had.

2

Nor does vision deny this: the province
of human discourse, error, self-delusion;
the spirit's oblique lifting a leverage
for the entire corpus; distressed paradigms;
and, as some have said, charges to answer.

How risible the solemnized
intentions towards joy.
Unexchangeable password, I have yet
to find the place appointed. It will come.

Over, across, the Pennine scarps and valleys
motorway lights – festal suspension bridge,
high-arching nocturne. I grasp the possible

rightness of certain things
that possess the imagination, however briefly;

the verdict of their patterned randomness.

On the Sophoclean Moment in English Poetry

A serene draw, the Sophoclean Moment
if only for a moment, issues thence
into the unforestalled or, failing that,
experienced inexperience. *Try again*
may itself be Sophoclean, who's to know.
I think, though, they mean plainer things by far,
but not basics precisely – not clay, schist,
quartz, Hornton greenstone. Words are never stone
except in their appearance. See me out,
long-domiciled epiphanies I trust.
Answer for what I am? No time to answer,
a nerve of ageing touched upon and primed:
as when the jittery leaf snags, is a mouse:
one stop from Sophocles to Sepulchre.

In the Valley of the Arrow

1

First flowers strike artificial at first sight,
the colours appear concocted, perhaps they are.
Crocus for starters soon looks pretty
much washed out.

Now here's real alchemy – the gorse
on roadside terraces, bristling with static,
spectator of its own prime, inclement challenge

or salutation brusquely in place,
hermetic at full display and rallying,

as best becomes it, spicy orator.

Not Bohemia, not Illyria, where dramatic virgins
immortalized as common grace rhetoric's
vernacular flowers. Still in your gift, dull stream,

the singing iron footbridges, tight weirs
pebble-dashed with bright water, a shivey blackthorn's
clouded white glass that's darker veined or seamed,

crack willow foliage, pale as a new fern,
silver-plated ivy in the sun's angle –

this for description's sake –
                        and, as the year
ploughs on, the massive briar, misshapen-
shouldered, gross, hairy, jigging with bees,

beata l'alma.

3

My shadow now resembles my father's: cloth
cap flat-planted with its jutty neb
that prods the leaf-litter. Ineffectually.

What do they think of while they think of nothing?
Thinks: check pulse-rate as last animus
jerks home – spit, spat – *they* of course being *them*.

The finite mind transcends its finitude
with the contrivance of affinities,
on the great wheel that keeps time in suspense.

Dying's no let-up, an atrocious
means of existence: nobody saved;
no sign of ransom if you comprehend me.

Smug bastard.

4

Heart-stab memento giving a side-glimpse
of feared eternity – left at the kiosk –
as on a bright path you might catch the shadow
of your attacker.

Sun off shields in middle distance
and lidded water saurian-scaled.

Standing or going there is always pain;
the machinations of set injuries;
sentiment in collusion with itself.

The wild geese racket and mute swans proceed
in formal agitation round the lake.

Not all his days are this eventful.

5

More than you know it's like dead trees that stay
the same, winter and summer – merds
to how he tells it – sheathed in samurai
mail of black ivy. At it again,

beata l'alma.

Unzipped and found addressing the smeared walls
of an underpass, crying not mý
address, no more unnamed accusers,

self-dubbed natural thespian enacts
age, incapacity – judge the witnesses –
brings himself off to video'd provocation.

Pardon my breathing.

Improvisations for Hart Crane

Thou canst read nothing except through appetite.

1

Super-ego crash-meshed idiot-savant.
And what háve you.
This has to be the show-stopper. Stay put.
Slumming for rum and rumba, dumb Rimbaud,
he the sortilegist, visionary on parole,
floor-walker watching space, the candy man,
artiste of neon, traffic's orator,
gaunt cantilevers engined by the dawn
of prophecy. A sight to see itself:
he, swinger with the saints in mission belfries,
broken and randy ringing up the toll.
Procrastination's death to be in time,
publish his name, exile's remittancer,
prodigal who reclaimed us brought to book.

2

The Stars-and-Stripes looks best when it's unfurled
stiff as a board on a declaiming wind
under a cobalt sky; the National
Guard at stand-to, half-tamed weaponry;
the Chief's advisers, unsexed white and black,
good with binoculars and shown to be so;
their photo-faces lit with simple purpose,
their public selves the sanctum, the arcane;
their privacy the secrets of events;
the keys of war bestowed like a small heirloom
of sentimental value to the clan.
Poets are unstable, least to be trusted
with scripts of grand arraignment. All in all
you screwed us, Hart, you and your zany epic.

3

Unwise these thoughts high-spanned. A shade too much
Library of America, liberty
safe on the list, shiny-electric-gated,
sordor its new-old mansions. Heave him in –
'lyric confession slams the bunkum test' –
our self-accusing bard: naked bacardi
and sailors! Straight sex mothered him;
for the witch he performed. I went along
with all that jazz, twizzled the fuzzy dial
to catch Roosevelt. Admit, though, we had plunged
before his first term, faithful old depression
working us all the way. What derelicts
we must have been, ripped off by infancy.
Thou canst grasp nothing except through appetite.

In Ipsley Church Lane 3

One solstice has swung past, the immeasurably
varied, unvarying, profusion of hedge-burgeon
stays richly dulled, immoveable for a while.
Over by Studley the close air is dove-grey,
a hollow without sun
though heat had filled it; shadow-reservoir,

more than a mirage, however you chance to look,
if mirage-like in its reality.
The day does not wear well, the well-kept grounds
of the new offices are uninviting.
There is a kind of sullenness that summer
alone possesses. It passes; will have passed:

not to speak of your heart, that rules and lies
in webs of heavy blood, a clobbering fetish.
Parables come to order; the hurt
is mortal though endurances remain,
as they have to, insufferably so;
hindsight and foresight stationed in their ways.

Offertorium: Suffolk, July 2003
for Annie and Julian

Even in a sparse county there is dense settling
and an unsettling that surfaces here or here
via the low levels, the tide-spiked rivers,
lanesides over-endowed by sovereign fern,
the crowned stalks I call hemlock, with poppies'
                                mass vagrancy,
rough forms of mallow, roses' battered shells.
A woodpigeon hauls into late take off,
self-snatched from truck wheels. Abundant hazards,
being and non-being, every fleck through which
                        this time affords
unobliterate certainties ǀ hidden in light:

From the Annals

'Now pick up your motorbike and go to bed.'

I

Imperilled by a virgin's lack of nous,
and she a Presbyterian in love,
too generous when encountering the world's ways
ex machina – motor so opportune,
like clockwork, chauffeused by a butch young thug
(her low Lugerian accent); gräfin in back
dispensing chloroform out of her furs.
(Changes in continuity my credit.)
Slightly obtuse those Viking-blooded gaels,
magnificent auxiliaries, who emerge
snorting their cosmic roles as engineers
with beards of cotton-waste and most chaste oaths.
Caesar himself dictates the signal flags
proud, choppy, flown at regulation height.

II

Metaphysics of physics: what is the secret
that nothing turns on though around it
everything circulates, the pull of this
interminable grey light in focused séance?
No intermission as the shock flotilla
moves to a change of course with spray-clawed bows.
Strike a good posture, comrade; time the reel.
Playing myth-bound, pure spirit that you are,
feign mind and soul like eerie Harpo Marx,
wiped off the celluloid, all watches primed
to set and match, a day saved by default
just as I said it would be. Gallant old tub
founders with an immediate deep upsurge.
Musical flotsam churns post-mortem Elgar.

No, no, no. Metaphysics of chemistry –
mystery play of the synapses for Veidt
and dominatrix Hobson. But play it as
convention's act of war. Is it possible
to love two men at once? I'd have said not
but this confounds me and is worth the price.
Passionate timing – saved by the torpedo.
(Error in detail there; write me about it,
you whacking bore. I yield to my invention.)
I've yielded to much else; and few are drawn
well purged into senescence. I should guess
that Iron Cross (2nd Class) is their mistake.
And what an exit-line – *It was my own*
boat that sank us – splendid! And valedictions.

Broken Hierarchies

When to depict rain – heavy rain – it stands
in dense verticals diagonally lashed,
chalk-white yet with the chalk translucent;

the roadway sprouts a thousand flowerets,
storm-paddies instantly reaped, replenished,
and again cut down:

the holding burden of a wistaria
drape amid drape, the sodden
copia of all things flashing and drying:

first here after the storm these butterflies
fixed on each jinking run,
probing, priming, then leaping back,

a babble of silent tongues;
and the flint church also choiring
into dazzle

. . .

like Appalachian music, those
aureate stark sounds
plucked or bowed, a wild patience

replete with loss,
the twankled dulcimer,
scrawny rich fiddle gnawing;

a man's low voice that looms out of the drone:
the humming bird that is not
of these climes; and the great

wanderers like the albatross;
the ocean, ranging-in, laying itself
down on our alien shore.

The Storm

(after Eugenio Montale, 'La Bufera')

The storm that batters the magnolia's
impermeable leaves, the long-drawn drum roll
of Martian thunder with its hail

(crystal acoustics trembling in your night's lair
disturb you while the gold transfumed
from the mahoganies, the pages' rims
of de luxe books, still burns, a sugar grain
under your eyelid's shell)

lightning that makes stark-white the trees,
the walls, suspending them –
interminable instant – marbled manna
and cataclysm – deep in you sculpted,
borne now as condemnation: this binds you
closer to me, strange sister, than any love.
So, the harsh buskings, bashing of castanets
and tambourines around the spoilers' ditch,
fandango's foot-rap and over all
some gesture still to be defined . . .
                                        As when
you turned away and casting with a hand
that cloudy mass of hair from off your forehead

gave me a sign and stepped into the dark.

Luxe, Calme et Volupté

to PMH

Lost is not vanished; nor is it finished;
more like a haunting from the ghosted future
that was not ours and cannot now be called
through into being by too late consent.
Motions towards life are not living
except abstractly I am moved to say.
Both of us here conjoined in epitaph
awaiting stone.

Improvisation on 'Warum ist uns das Licht gegeben?'

Scored by folk-genius set to its lathe.
I also am a worker in iron.
Patience be judge, nailers and puddlers,
chained free citizens, battling cortèges,
beyond subsistence, given that you are mine,
hammered to fable as in blood proven.
Against survival something that endures:
win, lose, the paid-up quiet death.